One Night in Bethlehem

Written by Tim Wesemann
Illustrated by Paul Reising

www.CTAinc.com

ISBN 1-933234-13-X
Printed in Thailand

One night in Bethlehem . . .

...families prayed for a Savior.

One night in Bethlehem
animals ate peacefully
from their mangers.

One night in Bethlehem storekeepers closed their shops at the end of a long day.

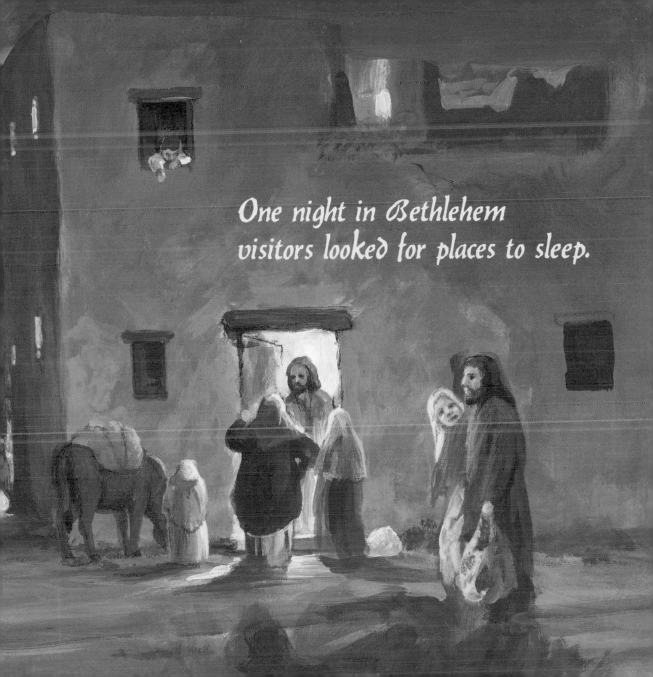

One night in Bethlehem
visitors looked for places to sleep.

One night in Bethlehem
the tax men counted money.

One night in Bethlehem
children slept in warm, comfy beds.

One night in Bethlehem shepherds watched their sheep in the meadow.

One night in Bethlehem
the moon and stars lit up the sky.

One night in Bethlehem
God had very special plans.

One night in Bethlehem
the angels of heaven were filled with happiness.

One night in Bethlehem
a baby was born to
Mary and Joseph.

One night in Bethlehem
a baby named Jesus was born.

One very special night in Bethlehem
the world changed . . .
because Jesus was
born for you!

And it came to pass in those days, that there went out a decree from Caesar Augustus, that all the world should be taxed. (And this taxing was first made when Cyrenius was governor of Syria.) And all went to be taxed, every one into his own city.

And Joseph also went up from Galilee, out of the city of Nazareth, into Judaea, unto the city of David, which is called Bethlehem; (because he was of the house and lineage of David:) To be taxed with Mary his espoused wife, being great with child. And so it was, that, while they were there, the days were accomplished that she should be delivered. And she brought forth her firstborn son, and wrapped him in swaddling clothes, and laid him in a manger; because there was no room for them in the inn.

And there were in the same country shepherds abiding in the field, keeping watch over their flock by night. And, lo, the angel of the Lord came upon them, and the glory of the Lord shone round about them: and they were sore afraid. And the angel said unto them, Fear not: for, behold, I bring you good tidings of great joy, which shall be to all people. For unto you is born this day in the city of David a Saviour, which is Christ the Lord. And this shall be a sign unto you; Ye shall find the babe wrapped in swaddling clothes, lying in a manger.

And suddenly there was with the angel a multitude of the heavenly host praising God, and saying, Glory to God in the highest, and on earth peace, good will toward men.

And it came to pass, as the angels were gone away from them into heaven, the shepherds said one to another, Let us now go even unto Bethlehem, and see this thing which is come to pass, which the Lord hath made known unto us.

And they came with haste, and found Mary, and Joseph, and the babe lying in a manger. And when they had seen it, they made known abroad the saying which was told them concerning this child. And all they that heard it wondered at those things which were told them by the shepherds. But Mary kept all these things, and pondered them in her heart. And the shepherds returned, glorifying and praising God for all the things that they had heard and seen, as it was told unto them.

Luke 2:1–20